Lunch Box Notes

Lunch Box Notes

J.M. Smith

Rev. date: 06/20/2019

To order additional copies of this book, contact:
Xlibris
1-888-795-4274
www.Xlibris.com
Orders@Xlibris.com
797610

Dedicated to my husband

You are my soul mate, my hero, my protector, my best
friend and most of all God joined us together
And no one can keep us apart anymore.

Thank You for
being my Knight in
Shinning Armor
I LOVE YOU SO
MUCH Have a
wonderful day

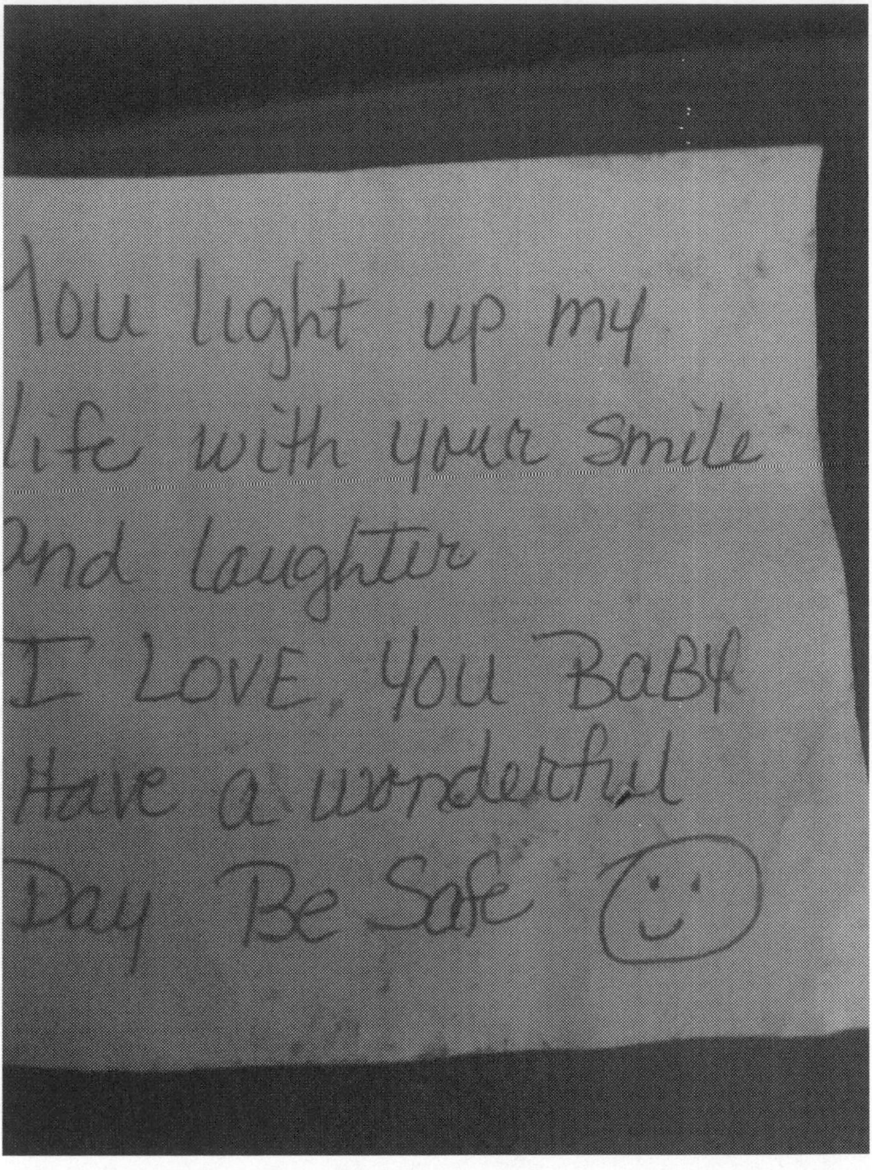
You light up my
life with your smile
and laughter
I LOVE YOU BABY
Have a wonderful
Day Be Safe

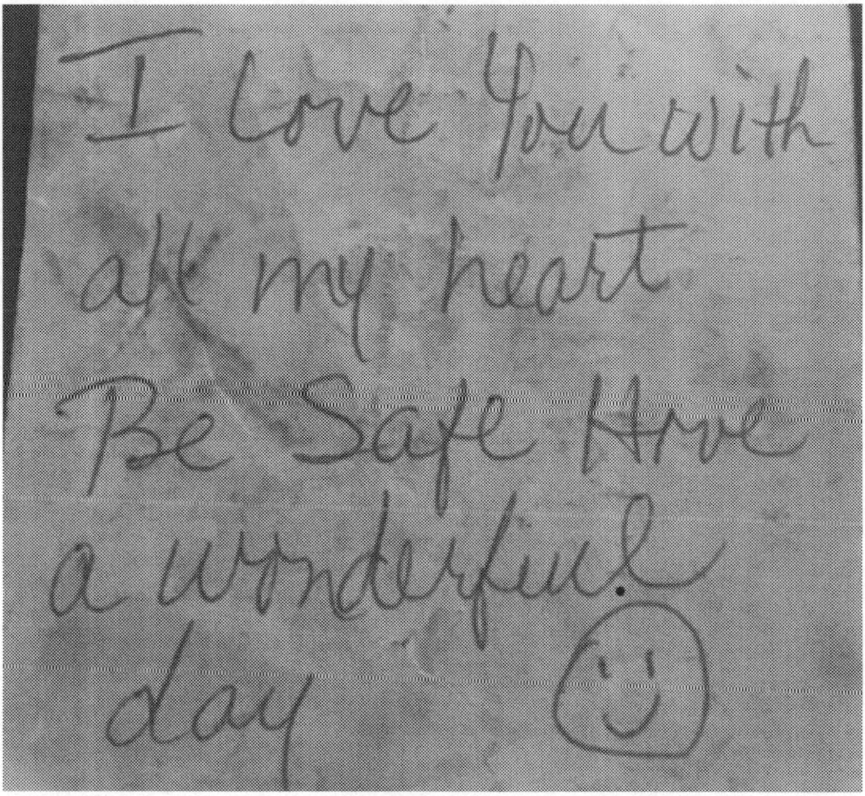
I love You with
all my heart
Be Safe Have
a wonderful
day

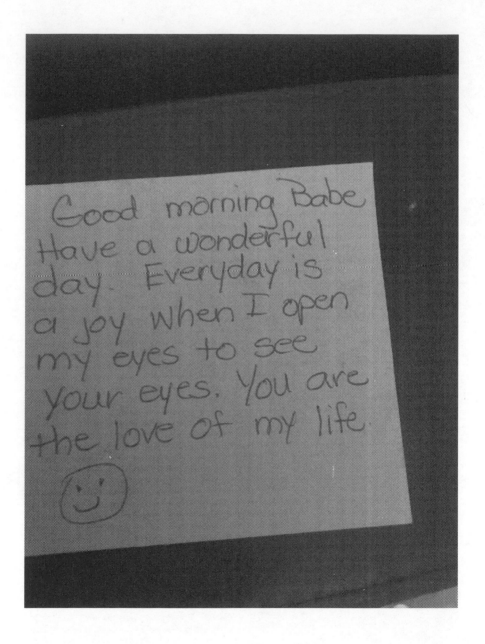

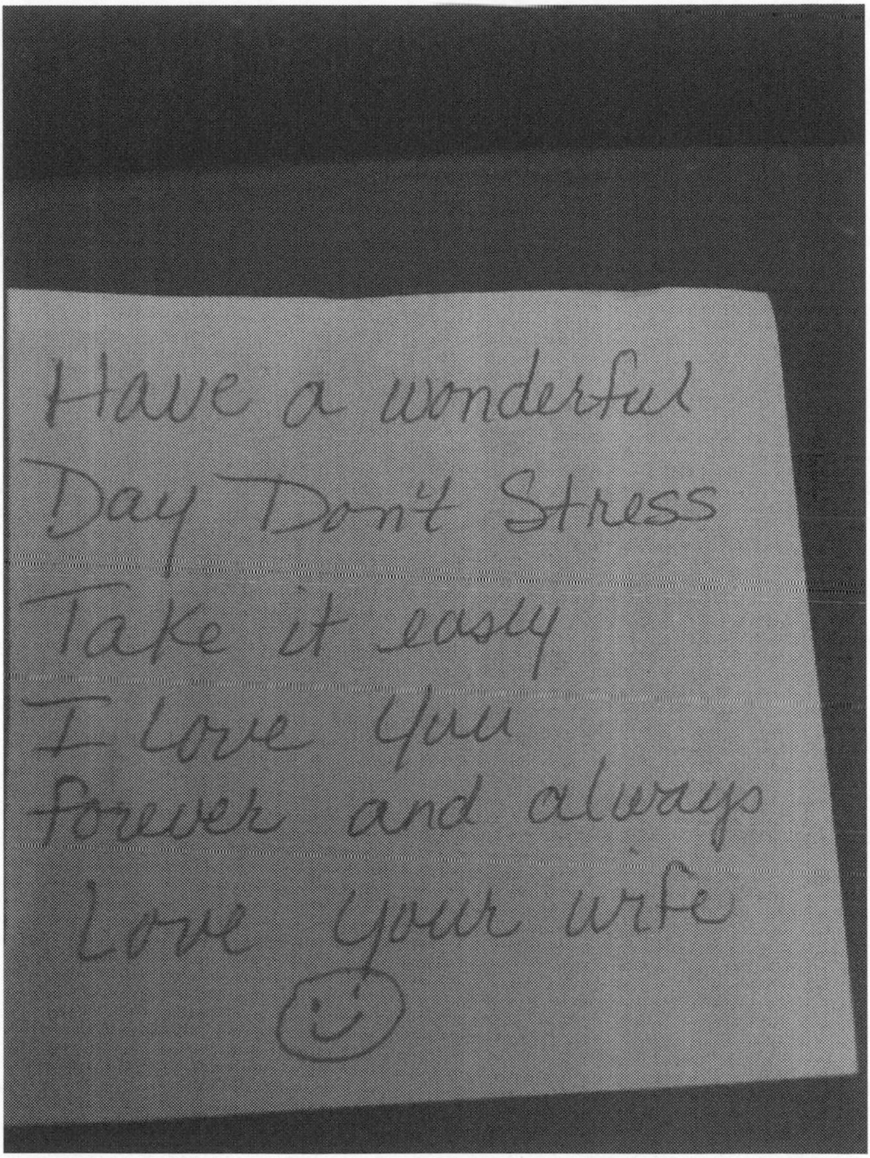
Have a wonderful
Day Don't Stress
Take it easy
I Love You
forever and always
Love your wife

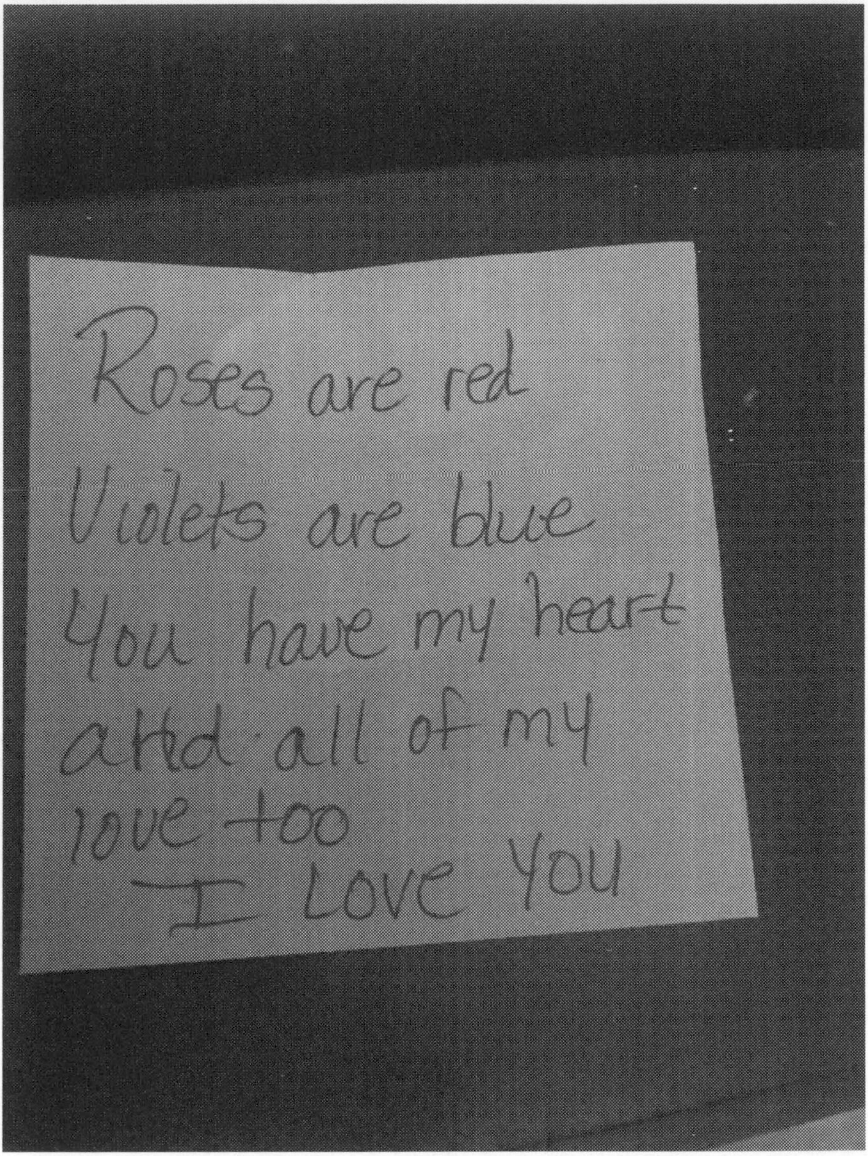
Roses are red
Violets are blue
You have my heart
and all of my
love too
I love you

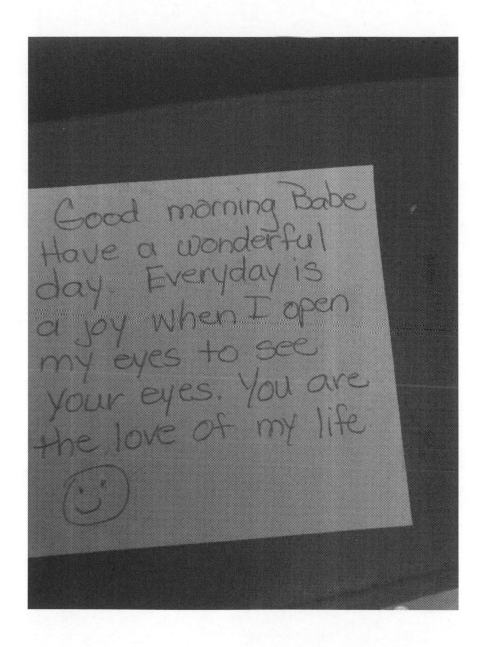

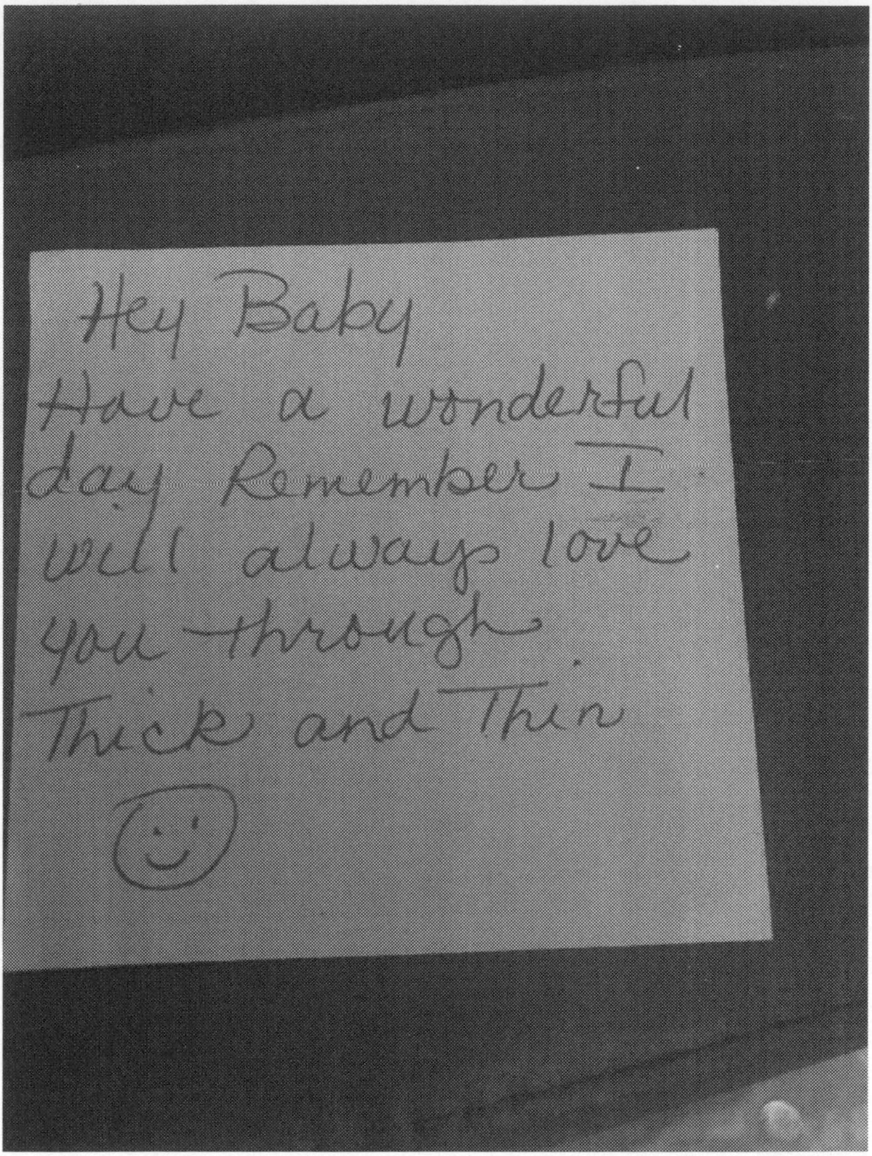
Hey Baby
Have a wonderful
day Remember I
will always love
you through
Thick and Thin

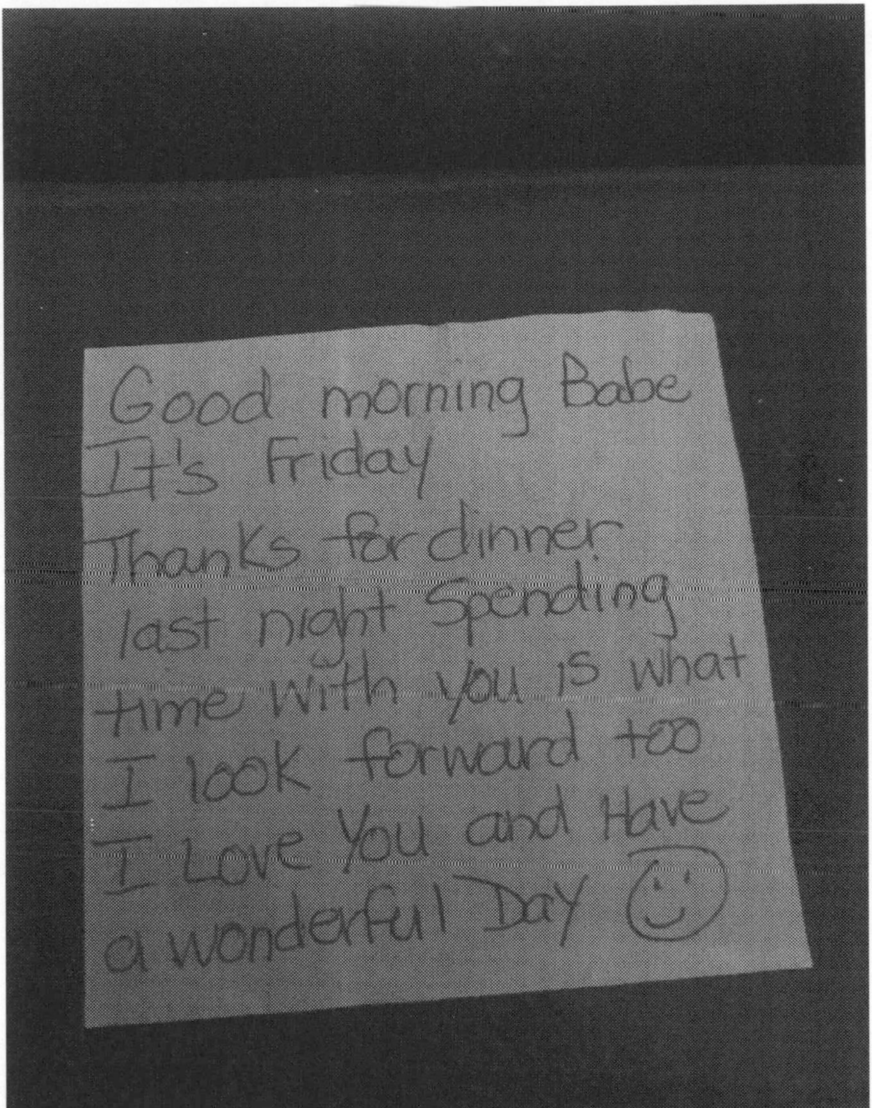
Good morning Babe
It's Friday
Thanks for dinner
last night Spending
time with you is what
I look forward too
I Love You and Have
a wonderful Day

Good morning my
Love
Hugs and Kisses
to you
You are my protector,
my best friend,
my soul mate, and
to be my husband
I Love You forever

Good morning Babe
Thank You for that
Wake up call this
morning. Nothing
like making love
in the morning
I Love You
Have a wonderful
Day

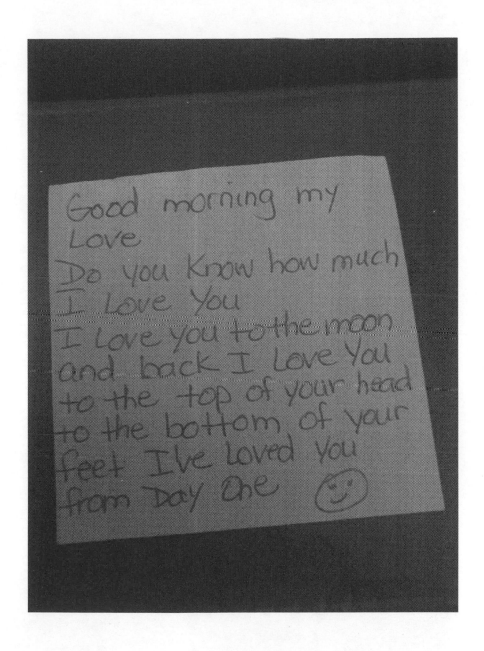

Good morning babe
Hope you slept well
Just sleeping next
to you, watching you,
and watching you
breath makes my
love get deeper every
day for you
Have a wonderful Day

Good morning Babe
You are a wonderful
man I Love you,
trust you, and brag
about you everywhere
I go I have the best
husband ever. Have
a wonderful day

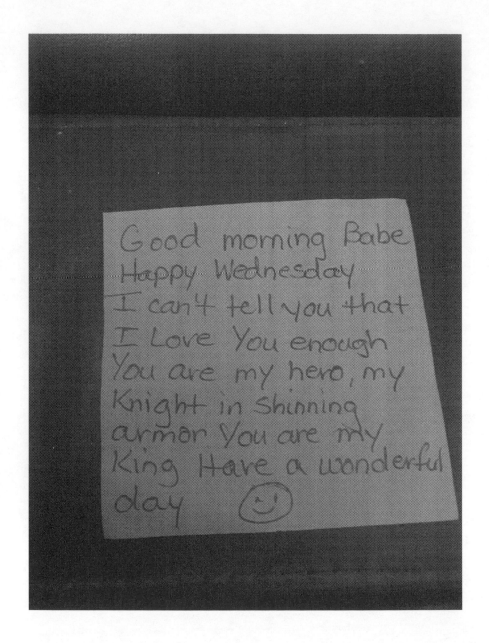

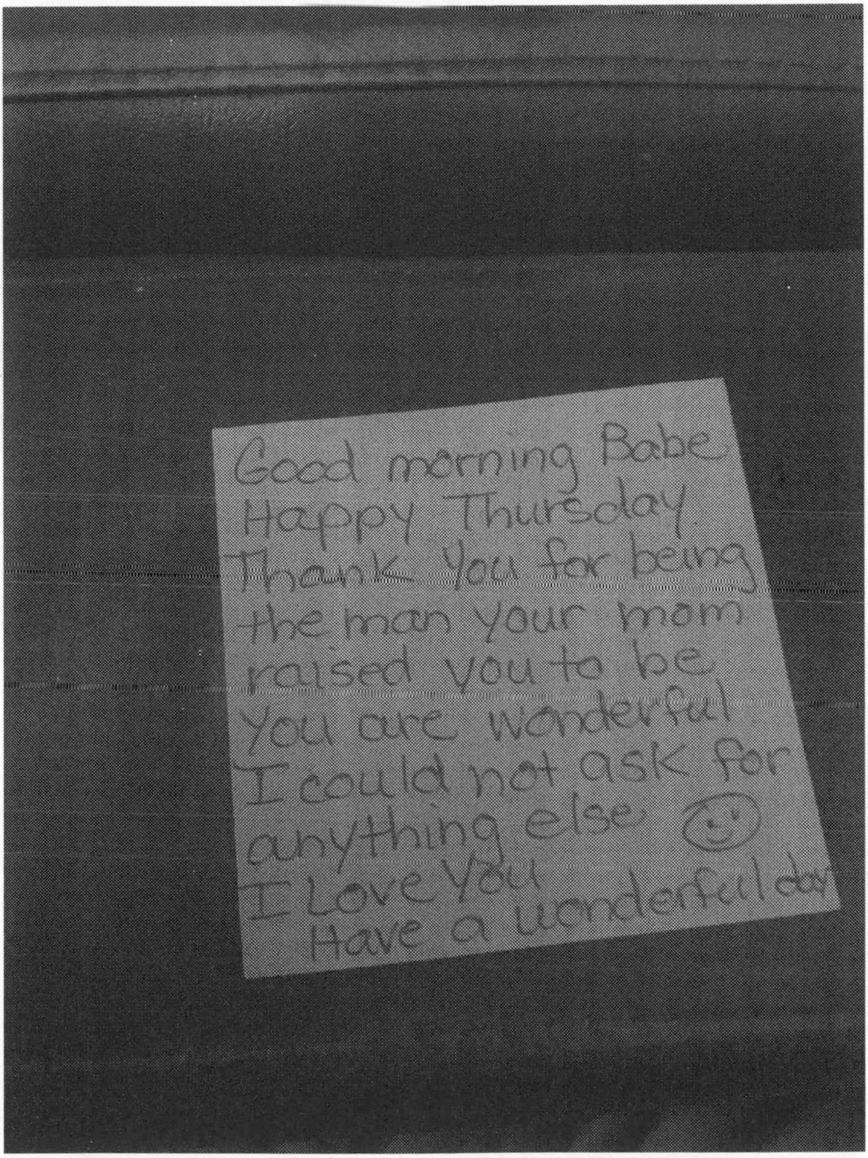
Good morning Babe
Happy Thursday
Thank You for being
the man your mom
raised you to be
You are wonderful
I could not ask for
anything else
I Love You
Have a wonderful day

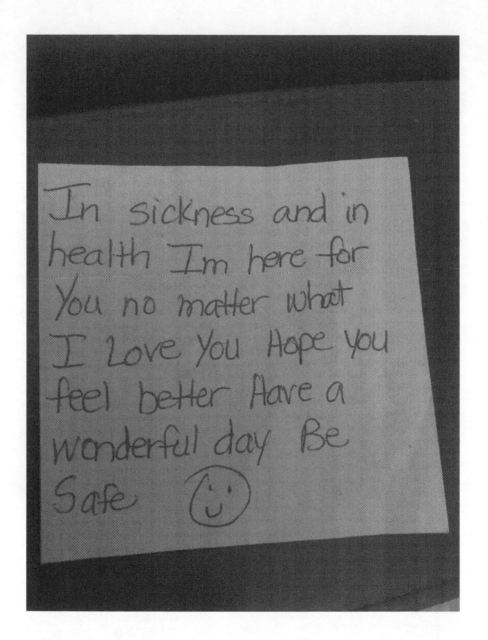

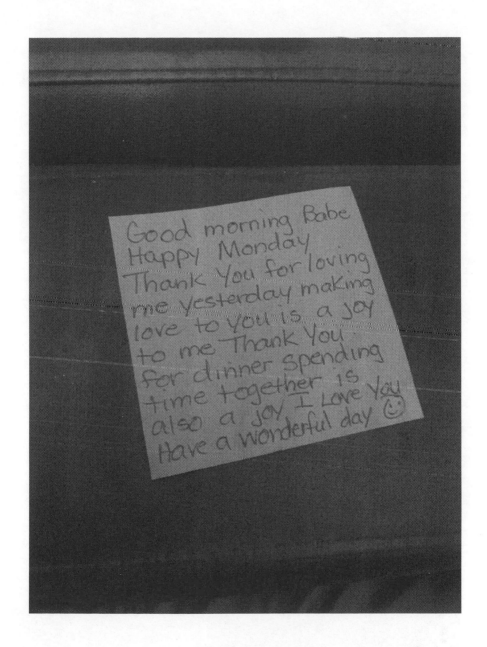

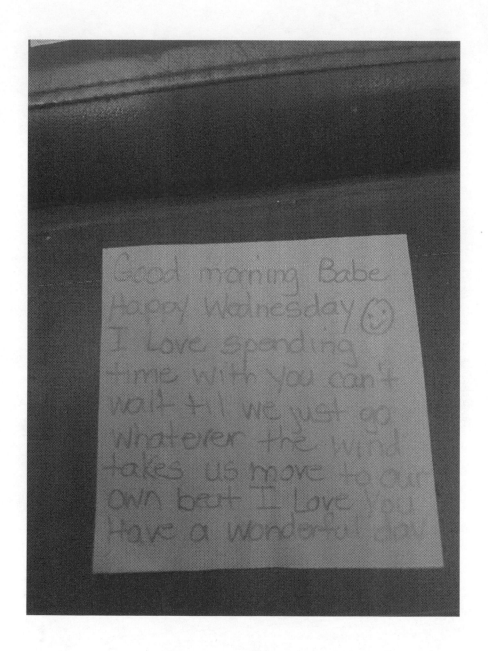

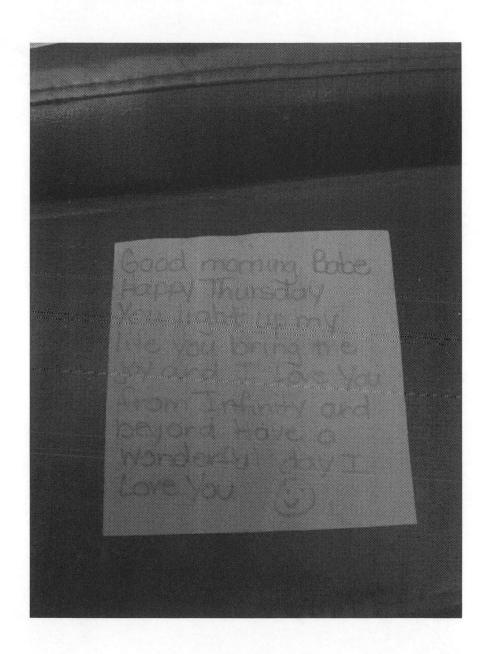

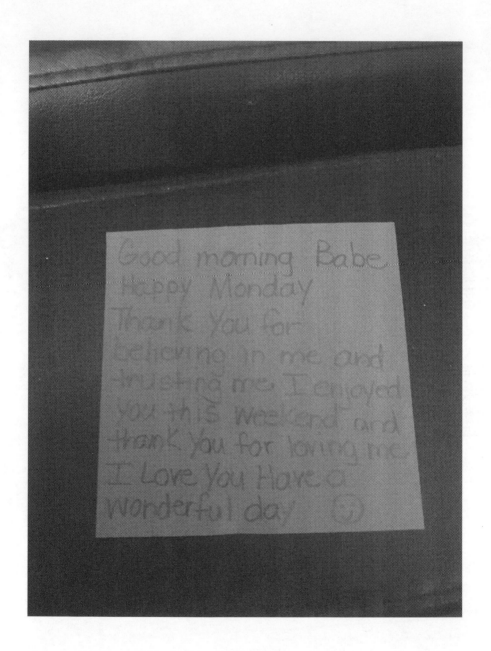

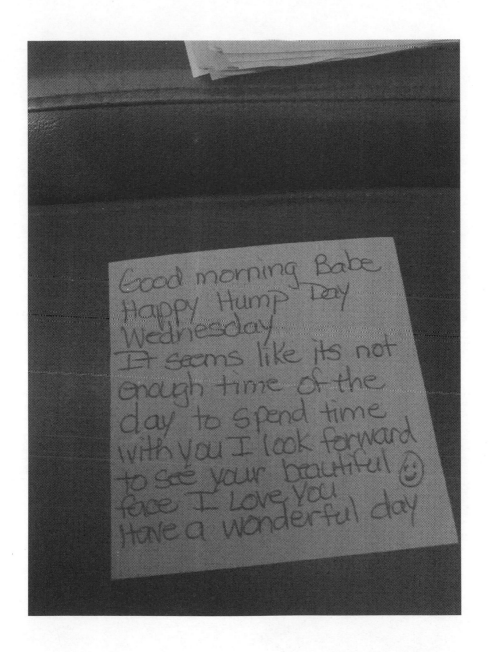

Good morning Babe
Happy Tuesday
You are my best
friend my soul mate
my protector my
lover and I Love
You with all my
heart Have a
wonderful day

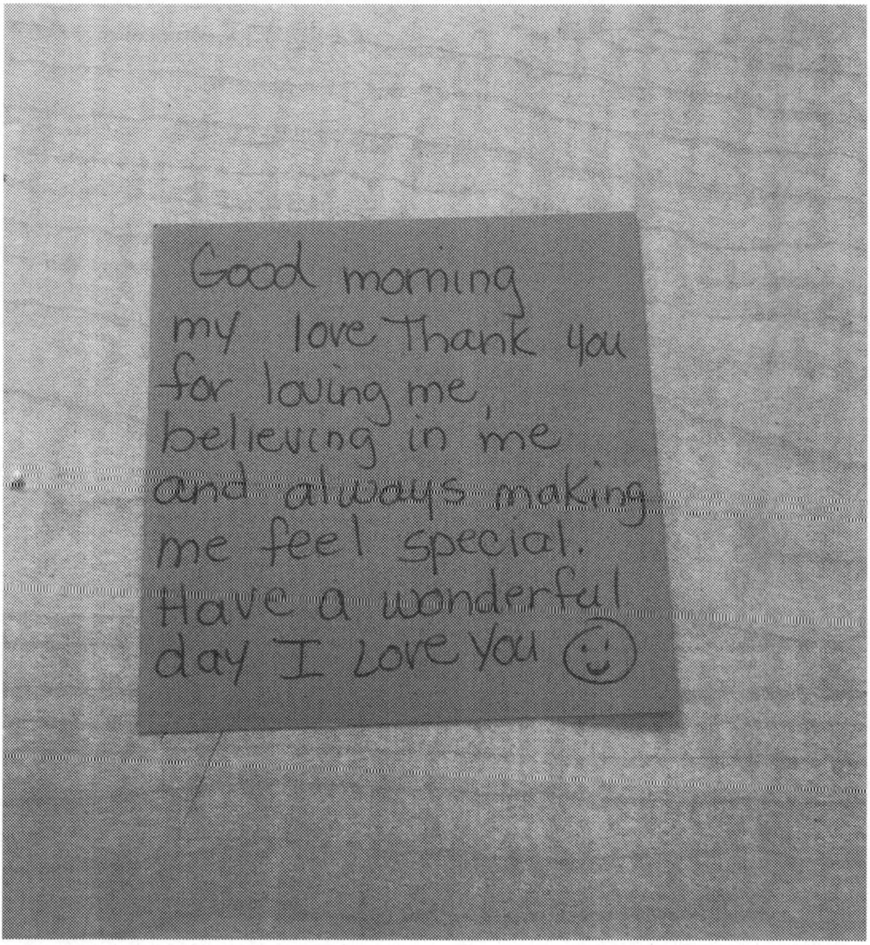
Good morning
my love Thank you
for loving me,
believing in me
and always making
me feel special.
Have a wonderful
day I Love You

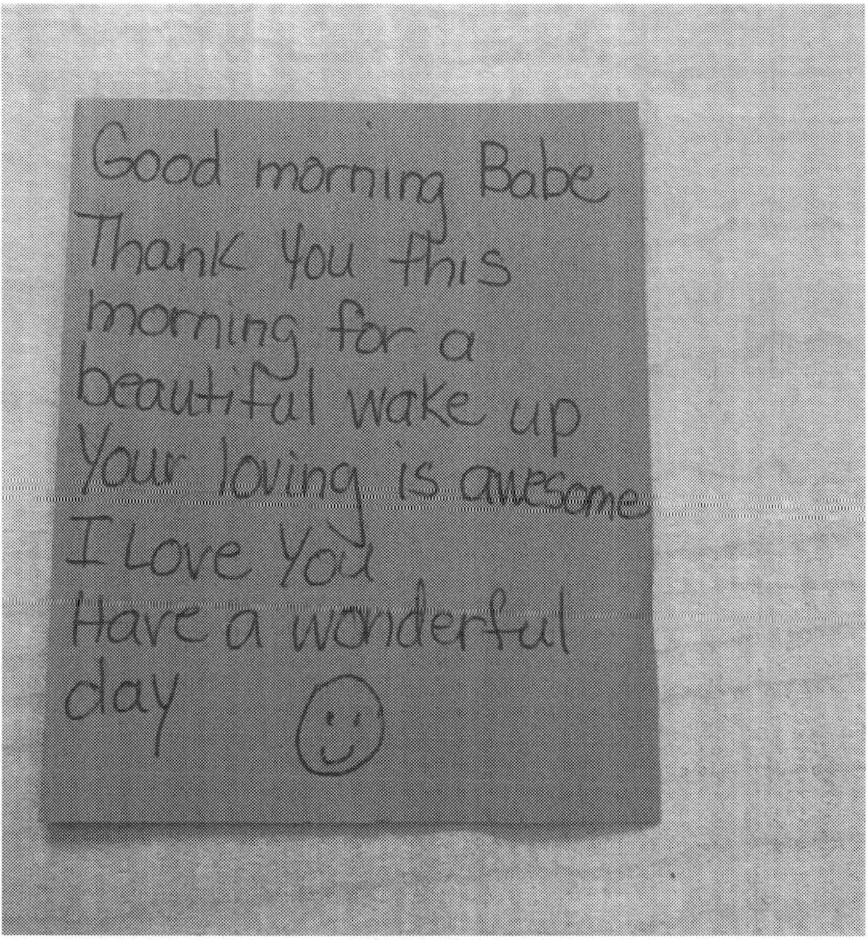
Good morning Babe
Thank You this
morning for a
beautiful wake up
Your loving is awesome
I Love You
Have a wonderful
day

Good morning Babe
You are the sun
in my sunshine
You light up my life
When I see your
beautiful smile
I Love you so much
Have a wonderful day

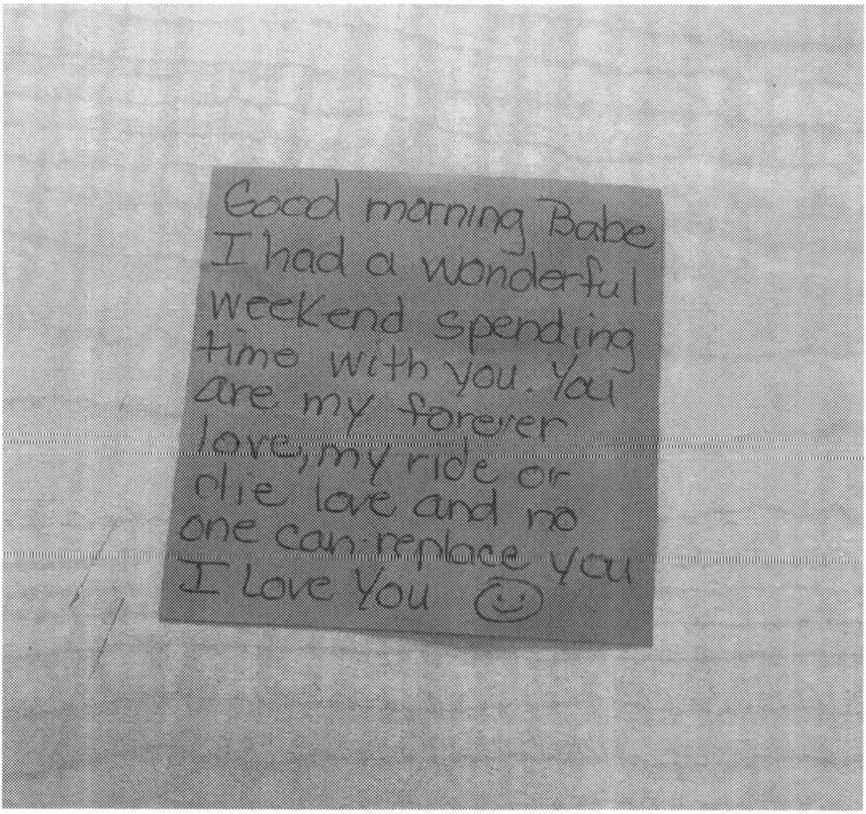
Good morning Babe
I had a wonderful
weekend spending
time with you. You
are my forever
love, my ride or
die love and no
one can replace you
I Love You

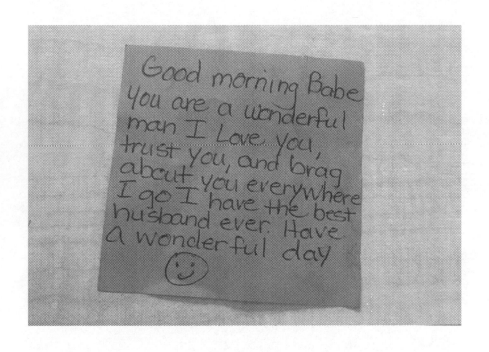

Good morning Babe
Happy Wednesday
I can't tell you that
I Love You enough
You are my hero, my
Knight in Shinning
armor You are my
King Have a wonderful
day

Good morning Babe
Happy Thursday
Thank You for being
the man your mom
raised you to be
You are wonderful
I could not ask for
anything else
I Love You
Have a wonderful day

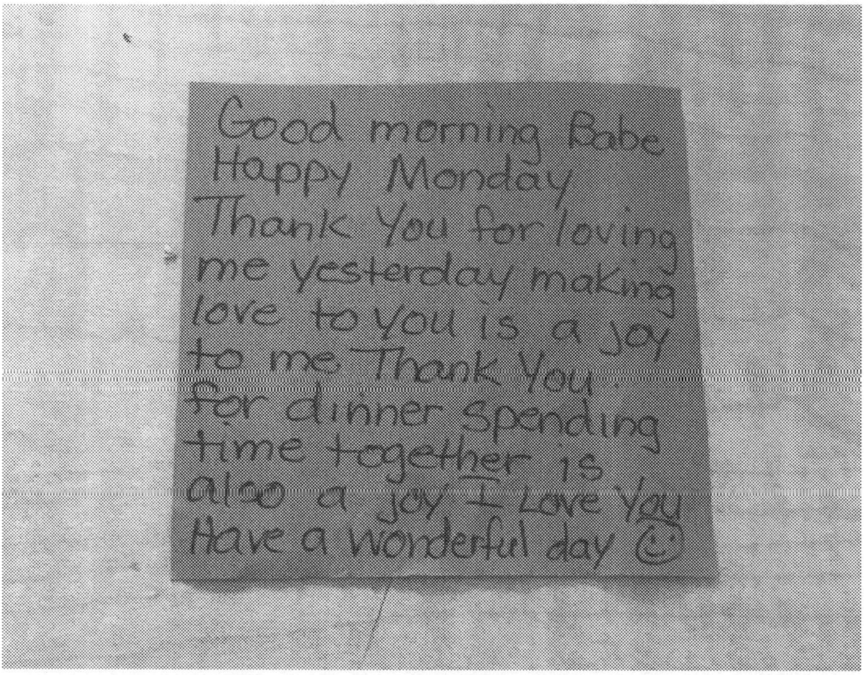
Good morning Babe
Happy Monday
Thank You for loving
me yesterday making
love to you is a joy
to me Thank You
for dinner spending
time together is
also a joy I Love You
Have a wonderful day

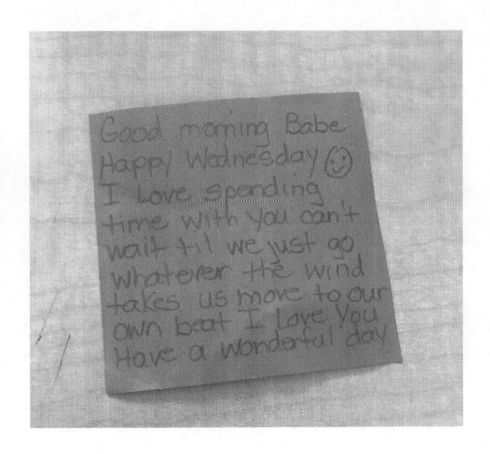

Good morning Babe
Happy Thursday
I Love You so much
You are my first love
I've loved you since
I was a teenager
Now God has brought
us together.
Have a wonderful day
☺

Good morning Babe
Happy Tuesday
You are my best
friend my soul mate
my protector my
lover and I Love
You with all my
heart Have a
Wonderful day

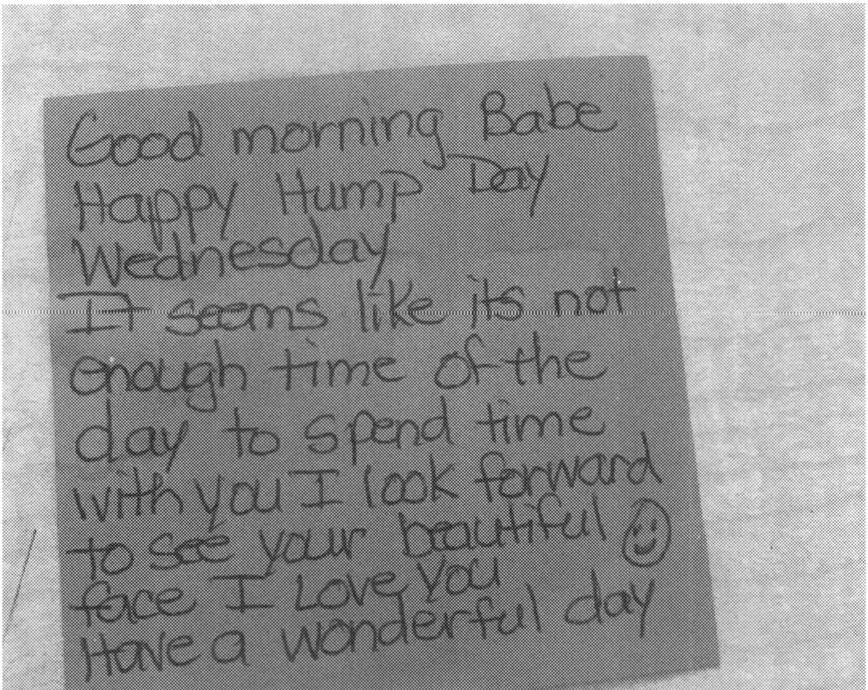
Good morning Babe
Happy Hump Day
Wednesday
It seems like its not
enough time of the
day to spend time
with you I look forward
to see your beautiful
face I Love You
Have a wonderful day

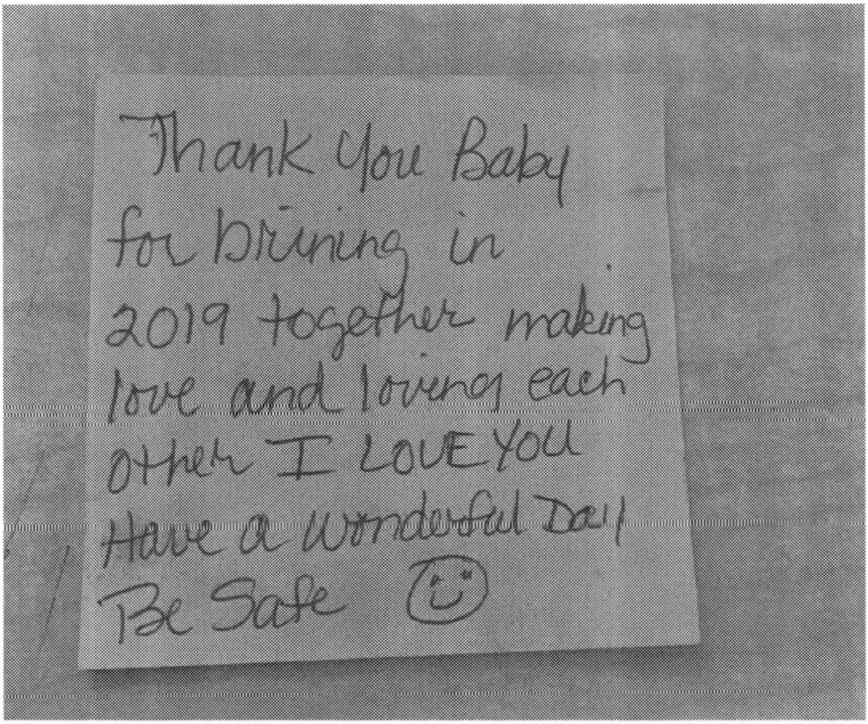
Thank You Baby
for brining in
2019 together making
love and loving each
other I LOVE YOU
Have a Wonderful Day
Be Safe

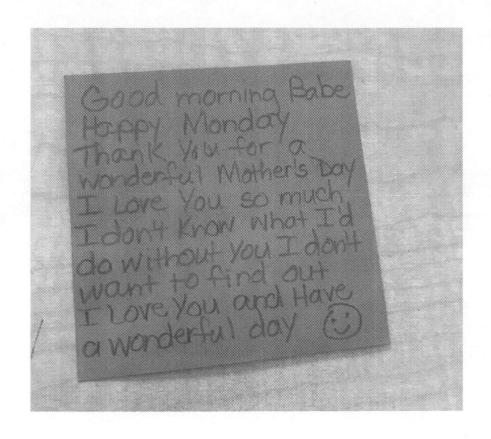

Good morning Babe
Happy Tuesday
I love waking up
next to you each
morning Starting the
day off seeing your
handsome face and
that beautiful Smile
I LOVE YOU Have a
wonderful Day

Good morning Babe
Happy Thursday
Next to God you are
my everything I
pray for you everyday
and thanking him
for bringing you in
my life I Love You
Have a wonderful
day

cause you are
my charm everything
I prayed for God
answered I Love
You so much to the
moon and back
Have a wonderful
day (☺)

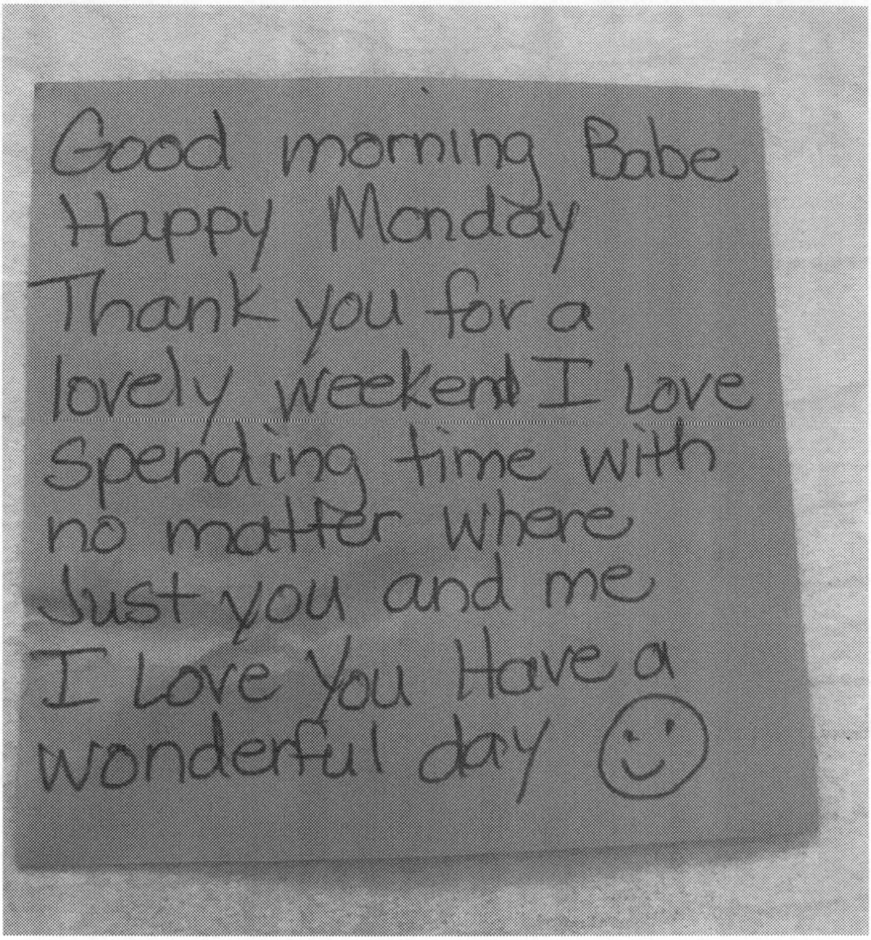
Good morning Babe
Happy Monday
Thank you for a
lovely weekend I Love
Spending time with
no matter where
Just you and me
I Love You Have a
wonderful day

Good morning Babe
Happy Tuesday
I Love hearing and
recieveing your phone
calls just to hear
your voice Thanking
God each day for you
I Love You Have a
wonderful day

Good morning Babe
Happy Wednesday
God put us together
to love one another
I would never put
you somewhere you
don't belong I
Love You Have
a wonderful day

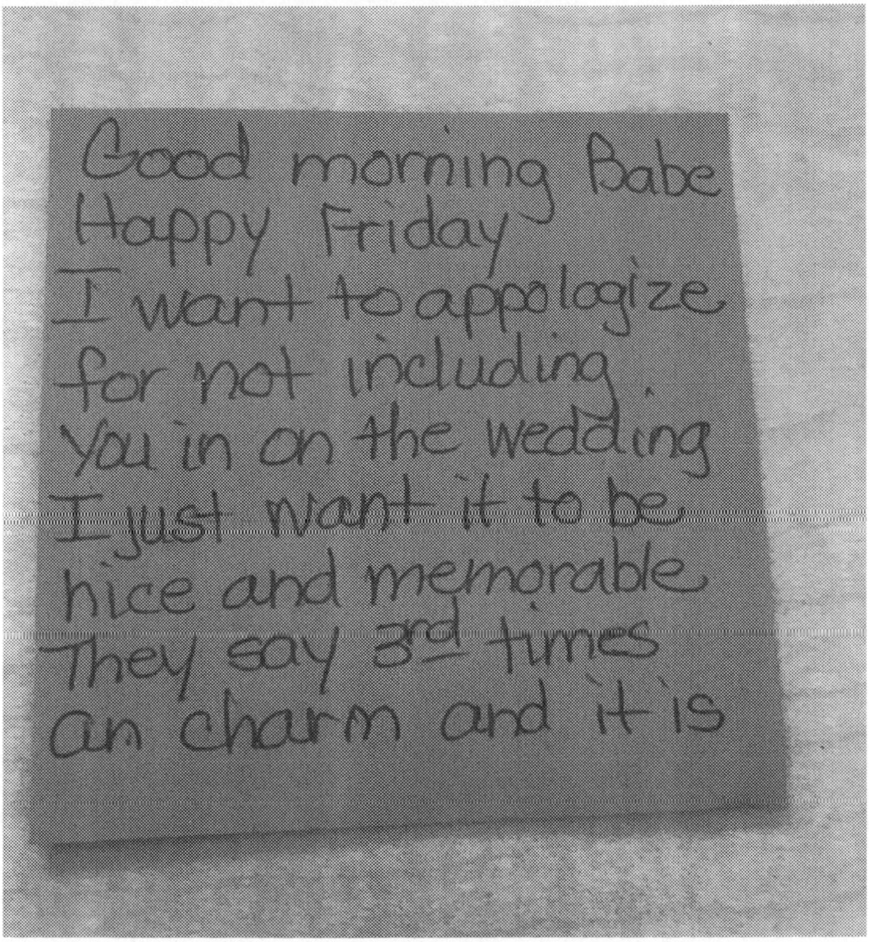
Good morning Babe
Happy Friday
I want to appologize
for not including
You in on the wedding
I just want it to be
nice and memorable
They say 3rd times
an charm and it is

Good morning Babe
Happy Thursday and
a Happy Thursday it
is I can't wait to
spend a wonderful
weekend with you
Just you and me
I Love You and Have
a wonderful day

Good morning Babe
Happy Wednesday
God put us together
to love one another
and I Love you so
much I would never
hurt you or put you
some place you don't
belong Have a
wonderful day ☺

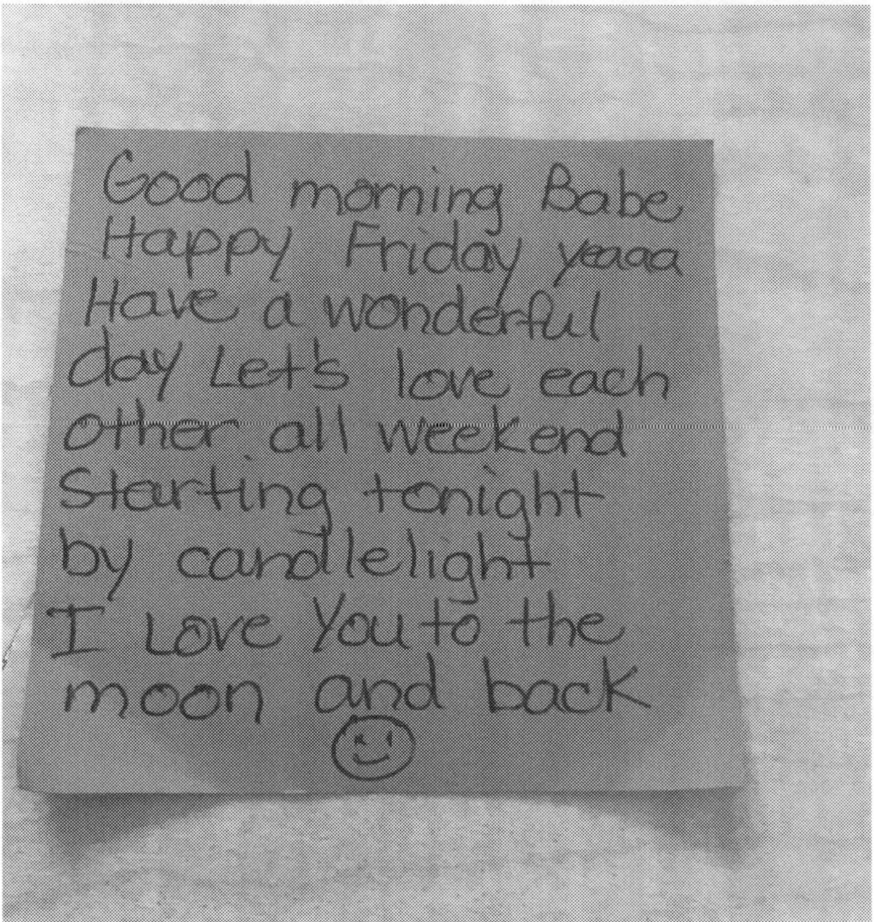
Good morning Babe
Happy Friday yeaaa
Have a wonderful
day Let's love each
other all weekend
Starting tonight
by candlelight
I Love You to the
moon and back

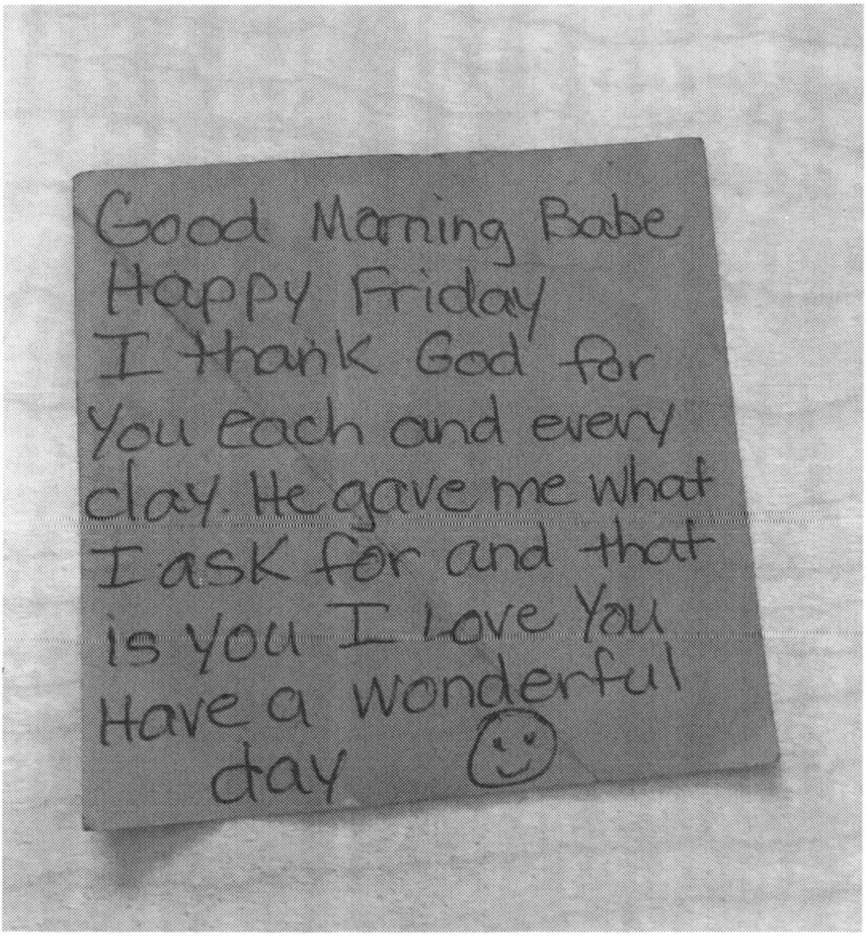
Good Morning Babe
Happy Friday
I thank God for
You each and every
day. He gave me what
I ask for and that
is you I Love You
Have a wonderful
day